flower
arranging

flower
a r r a n g i n g

Mandy Edwards and Eileen Nott N.D.S.F. F.S.F
with Gillian Haslam

p

Eileen Nott and **Mandy Edwards**, both very experienced florists, work together at Eileen Nott Florist, Tunbridge Wells, England. Eileen is a holder of the National Diploma, Society of Floristry and is a Fellow of the Society of Floristry. She is also a national judge for *Interflora*. **Gillian Haslam** is an experienced editor and writer, specialising in crafts, cookery, interiors, and gardening.

This is a Parragon Publishing Book

This edition published in 2006

Parragon Publishing
Queen Street House
4 Queen Street
Bath BA1 1HE, UK

Designed, produced and packaged by Stonecastle Graphics Limited
Cover design by Fiona Roberts

Floral designs and arrangements by Mandy Edwards and Eileen Nott N.D.S.F, F.S.F
Text by Gillian Haslam
Edited by Philip de Ste. Croix
Designed by Sue Pressley and Paul Turner
Photography by Roddy Paine
Flowers and equipment supplied by Eileen Nott Florist, Tunbridge Wells, England

ISBN 1-40546-383-X

Printed in China.

Candle safety

Although candles and flowers are perfect partners, to use candles safely always follow the following safety instructions:

• Always read carefully the warning instructions supplied with the candles.

• Always ensure candles are anchored securely within the display so there is no danger of them toppling over.

• Never leave burning candles unattended or attempt to move them when lit.

• Make sure any flowers and foliage are arranged out of the flame's reach and extinguish well before the candle reaches the top of the decoration.

• Never leave fragments of a match or wick in the candle after lighting as they may create a dangerous second source of flame.

• Keep wicks well trimmed and burn away from walls and overhanging surfaces.

• Burn in an area free from draughts and away from flammable materials.

• Never allow a candle to continue to burn if the flame becomes enlarged.

contents

introduction

When it comes to turning a house into a home, flowers are one of those useful, instant design solutions. They immediately bring any room to life with their beautiful colors and glorious scent, giving it a welcome sense of homeliness. Just think of all those house makeover programs on television – flowers are always used to add that perfect finishing touch to a room that's undergone a radical transformation.

Whatever your chosen look for your home – be it sleekly modern and minimalist or a cosy cottage theme, or any of the hundreds of styles in between – you can use flowers to bring a room to life. The displays featured in this book have been devised to suit every style of room.

Unfortunately all too often people buy or are given the most wonderful flowers but they are at a loss to know how to arrange or display them. The secret lies in just a few simple techniques and one or two pieces of essential equipment.

The projects that follow explain the techniques you need and show how to make the most of your flowers. The projects range from uncomplicated arrangements using flowers and foliage gathered from the garden that can be assembled in just a few minutes, to more formal table centers and party decorations that require a little more planning and forethought. You can either choose

to use the flowers and foliage listed for each project or, as you gain confidence, use the photographs of the finished arrangements as inspirational starting points and adapt the designs according to the flowers you have to hand. Some of the arrangements use just one or two blooms which means that it's possible to create something stunning even if you don't have many flowers to hand.

You will also discover that there is more to a successful arrangement than simply a good selection of flowers. Foliage, moss, grasses, and twigs are equally important. Even during long winter months you'll find that garden greenery can be used to great effect with the addition of shop-bought blooms. So now's the time to dust off the vases, sharpen the shears, and start arranging!

flowers in your home

*T*o get the best out of the flowers you arrange for your home and to create displays that will last for more than just a day or two, it's important to follow a few simple guidelines when choosing flowers at a florist's shop or when picking them from your own garden. There are also a few 'tricks of the trade' that many professional florists use to ensure the blooms stay at their best for as long as possible.

choosing flowers

Choosing the best flowers possible is the first stage in creating a beautiful arrangement, but it can be a little bewildering knowing how to select the best bunches. Always ask the florist for advice – they deal with flowers day in, day out and are well versed in the performance and demands of each variety. Explain the type of arrangement you have in mind and its intended location and listen to what they recommend. For instance, it is not always best to buy flowers that are still in tight buds as they may never fully open. Similarly, flowers that are already in full bloom may fade and die very quickly when placed in a warm room. If you buy flowers regularly, you will soon build up a wealth of knowledge.

Always keep your eyes open for unusual varieties that you haven't used before. Ask the florist's advice about how to care for them, then take them home and create something fabulous with them!

caring for flowers

When you get your flowers home, don't be in a rush to arrange them. The first task is to trim all the stems diagonally (to create a larger surface area for taking up water and nutrients) and to give them a long drink in a bucket of water. Use a sharp knife to cut the stems as scissors tend to bruise and crush them. There is no need to crush the woody stems of flowers such as roses as this only encourages the spread of bacteria.

If gathering flowers and foliage from the garden, try to pick them early in the morning when they are at their freshest. Never pick them when the sun is at its strongest. Give flowers a good drink of water and submerge the foliage in a bucket of cool water. This revives the leaves and helps them to retain their glossy green coloring (the only exception to this rule is gray-leaved foliage which loses its color if plunged underwater).

color theory

Color is one of the most exciting aspects of flower arranging and can create an immediate impact. The color wheel illustrated below shows how the different rainbow shades work together, which ones harmonize and which ones create contrasts.

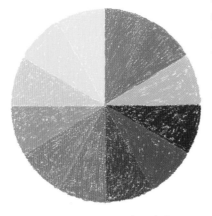

The color wheel shows the relation-ship between different colors and how they tone and contrast.

Choose your flower colors with care. For a subtle arrangement, choose flowers with a toning range of colors, perhaps from soft blues through to strong purples. For a more eye-catching display that demands to be looked at, choose colors from the hotter end of the spectrum – an arrangement of fiery reds and sunset oranges will never fade into the background.

Unlike other forms of interior decoration, flower arranging allows you to experiment with unusual combinations of colors. Let your imagination run riot and don't be afraid to try something new – you may stumble across a stunning color mix and if a color scheme doesn't work, it's an easy business to rearrange the flowers.

shape and form

Flowers can be divided into three main shape categories. The first comprises round or focal flowers, for example roses, ranunculi, and gerberas. Tall flowers, such as delphiniums, irises, lilies, or gladioli, are known as line materials. Within a display, these two very different shapes are often linked by softer, flowing transitional shapes, such as carnations or lisianthus. When selecting the flowers for a large arrangement, it's worth bearing these guidelines in mind as they will help you to give a good balance to the overall structure.

You will see from the various projects in this book that the tall stems are often placed first, to give a strong framework for the display, and the softer or more rounded flowers are then used to fill in and add body to the arrangement.

equipment

*O*ne of the great things about flower arranging is that you can begin with the absolute minimum of equipment. Unlike some crafts which require a major investment in terms of tools and materials, here you can start off simply with a sharp knife, a clean vase, and a bunch of flowers. However, there are some things which will make life easier and help you to create more unusual arrangements.

essentials

A sharp knife is the one essential you really can't do without. Use it for trimming stems cleanly and for cutting floral foam. A knife with a short blade is easiest to handle. Shears are useful for cutting flowers and foliage from the garden, but

make sure the blades are kept sharp and in good condition. It's better to use a knife, rather than shears, for cutting stems to achieve a cleaner cut.

Wires can be very handy in flower arranging. They can be used to

support flowers with weak stems and to coax flowers into position within a display. Wires are available in different thicknesses (or gauges) and are either sold in straight lengths or on a reel. Use wire cutters to trim them to length (if you use scissors, the blades will soon become very blunt or misshapen). Wires can also be cut into short lengths and bent in half to form 'hairpins' which can be used to anchor moss or other coverings in position on floral foam.

floral foam

Floral foam in indispensable. It is available in two different forms – one specifically for dried flower arranging and one for use with fresh flowers, so make sure you buy the correct type. It is usually sold in easy-to-cut blocks or preformed into circles or wreath shapes.

Floral foam must be soaked thoroughly before use. To do this, float a block in a bowl of water and allow it to take up the liquid. Blocks of foam can be joined together or fixed to containers using special florist's adhesive tape.

choosing vases and containers

Containers can form the starting point for many arrangements and should be chosen with care. The main thing to avoid is a container which overwhelms the flowers or is too eyecatching – you want people to notice the flowers rather than their container.

Clear, plain glass is an obvious choice as it comes in so many shapes and sizes. It's useful to build up a collection of vases of varying heights and sizes and with different neck shapes. You can also use water jugs and drinking glasses to hold flowers to great effect. Always clean glass vases thoroughly to prevent watermarks forming and bacteria breeding which will shorten the life of an arrangement. Stubborn stains can usually be soaked away.

Also try to think beyond the obvious when choosing containers. Raid the kitchen cupboards for ceramic bowls, soup and vegetable tureens, metal cake tins, and so on. The only stipulation is to make sure they are watertight.

Use your imagination when selecting containers. Here flowers have been displayed to great effect within a glass vase and inside a metal cake tin.

ribbons and ties

Ribbons and ties can add the perfect finishing touch to a bouquet or vase arrangement, and they are available in such a glorious array of colors. Choose shades to match the blooms or to create a complete contrast.

Practice tying large bows with ribbon offcuts, and curl strips into ringlets by carefully running a length of ribbon across scissor blades.

As well as the traditional, fairly crisp florist's ribbon, try using colored or natural hessian ribbon (as shown on the left) to add a more modern touch to traditional bouquets or posies. Net ribbon with wired edges also presents great decorative possibilities as it can be tweaked into all sorts of wonderful shapes, which it will then retain.

Raffia or curling ribbon (a very narrow type of florist's ribbon) are often used for tying hand-held arrangements. This binding can then either be hidden with extra foliage within a vase display, or covered with more decorative ribbon and bows for a bouquet. If using colored raffia, be aware that its colors can bleed or stain if it becomes wet, which could discolor water in a vase arrangement of flowers.

using candles

Candles and flowers are a classic combination, the flickering light from the flames creating all sorts of interesting shadows and picking out the detail in the petals. Table centers are one obvious place to combine the two. They are the perfect way to dress up the table for a special meal.

Always make sure that candles are securely anchored within a display so there is no danger of them toppling over. Special holders (as shown on the left) can be used in conjunction with floral foam-based arrangements. These holders have a pointed base which sits snugly in the foam. The wreath-style arrangement on page 87 uses a fat pillar candle within a storm lantern – an extremely safe way to combine these two elements.

Remember never to leave lit candles unattended and always make sure they are fully extinguished at night. Don't place candles in a draft and make sure that any flowers and foliage are arranged out of the flame's reach. See page 4 for full safety instructions before using candle arrangments.

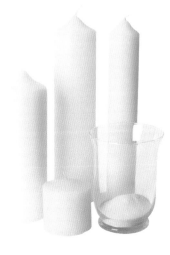

other useful materials

As well as flowers and foliage, use other materials to add color, shape and texture to your arrangements.

Colored sand and gravel are brilliant ways to bring interest to an otherwise plain container. They can also be used to raise the base of the container if the stems of your chosen flowers are too short for the vase you wish to use. Either use one single color, or carefully build up layers of contrasting shades for a striped effect. The trick when creating stripes is to employ a little patience. Allow one colored layer to settle before adding the next and trickle water into the vase slowly to prevent the colors mixing into one muddy mess.

Shells look fantastic lying on the base of a clear glass vase, the water making their opalescent colors shimmer and glisten. Polished pebbles and nuggets of glass and crystal can be used in a similar way inside a clear container, and can also be used to add interest to moss-covered floral foam, as on page 65.

Feathers add a touch of humor to flower displays. Look in haberdashery departments for feathers in all colors of the rainbow.

Moss is perfect for covering foam-based displays. It can easily be pinned in place with 'hairpins' made from bent lengths of wire. Mist with a water spray to keep it fresh.

Wispy, pure white feathers add a delicate touch to a bowl of tulips.

Layers of striped gravel and silver seashells add interest to a plain vase.

techniques and tips

*T*here are very few special techniques you need to
learn in order to create stunning displays, but it
is useful to master of few of the methods used by
professional florists. These will then allow you to
experiment with many different styles of arrangements.
Always handle flowers gently and try not to keep them
out of water for too long. Remember to let them have a
long drink of water before you start arranging them.

hand tying an arrangement

1 When creating a hand-tied arrangement, it is important to remember to
keep rotating the flowers within your hand to ensure that the posy looks
good from all angles. Strip the lower leaves from the stems. Hold the first
blooms in your hand and add a few pieces of foliage to one side.

2 Add a group of three or four
blooms of a different flower on
the other side of the foliage, holding
the posy tightly just below the
flower heads. The flowers will create
more impact when flowers of the
same species are grouped together,
rather than being separated.

3 Add another group of flowers with their heads at a slightly lower level, creating a domed effect.

4 Add more flowers, then surround them with a final outer layer of leafy foliage.

5 Secure the posy with a length of raffia tied tightly just below the flower heads and lower leaves.

6 Trim all the stems so they are of a fairly even length. Tweak any flowers if they are slightly out of position. Tie a thicker bundle of raffia around the stems to make a large decorative bow.

front-facing arrangement

This arrangement has an asymmetric, front-facing design (rather than an all-round design), but is also built up in the hand. It can either be used for a bouquet or for a vase display.

1 Begin by placing the tallest flowers in position to create an outline. This view is seen from the front.

2 Add more flowers and foliage at a lower level, making sure the asymmetric (or triangular) framework established by the taller stems is adhered to.

3 Bulk up the display, keeping within the overall shape. The view from the side, pictured here on the left, shows how all the flowers should face forward.

4 The finished design, viewed from the front, is shown here on the right.

bending snake grass

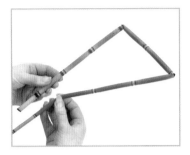
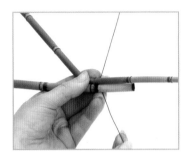

1 Snake grass is tremendously useful as it can be bent into various geometric shapes, as in the arrangement on page 75.

2 Hold the grass firmly in one hand and bend it gently into the required shape with the other. Take care not to snap it into pieces.

3 Bind the ends together firmly with a length of florist's wire or tie with raffia. The snake grass will hold the shape.

leaf folding

1 Aspidistra leaves are perfect for folding into gently curved arcs, as seen in the sunflower arrangement on page 55.

2 Hold the stem of one large leaf firmly in one hand and gently bend the leaf down. Pinch the tip of the leaf to the stem.

3 Bind the leaf tip to the stem with a short length of florist's wire. Wrap the wire around the leaf tip several times to make it secure.

wiring bear grass

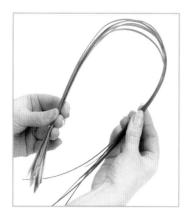

1 Wired strands of bear grass add a beautiful sculptural quality to flower arrangements.

2 Holding strands of grass in one hand, bend the tips over to form a small loop.

3 Bind them firmly together by wrapping a length of florist's wire around them several times.

4 Bend the tips upward to create a feathery frond. Take care not to snap them off.

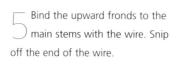

5 Bind the upward fronds to the main stems with the wire. Snip off the end of the wire.

pinning moss

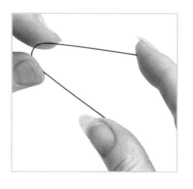

1 Pinned moss is ideal for hiding floral foam bases. Make the pins by bending short lengths of florist's wire into 'hairpin' shapes.

2 Place the moss in position and gently push a wire 'hairpin' through the moss into the foam to hold it secure.

joining twigs

1 Twigs can provide a wonderful framework for tall flower displays, as on page 37. Hold two twigs at right angles to each other.

2 Take a long length of raffia and bind it tightly in a crosswise fashion over the junction point of the two twigs.

3 Tie the two ends of the raffia together in a neat, firm knot and snip off the ends of the raffia close to the knot.

joining wire

 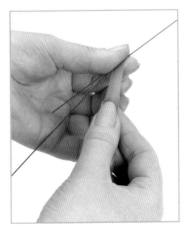 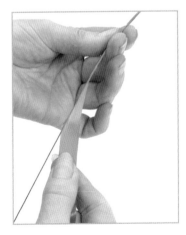

1 It can be necessary to join short lengths of wire to support taller flowers. Hold two wires side by side, slightly overlapping.

2 Wrap a length of florist's adhesive parafilm tightly around the two wires to bind them securely together.

3 If you wish, continue to wrap the entire length of the wire in parafilm. This will hide the join and make the wire sturdier.

Chapter 1
warm welcome

color sensation

*T*his mixed arrangement of summer blooms looks good from all angles, making it perfect for display on a central table. It is made by holding the flowers in one hand, adding the stems one at a time, constantly twisting the bunch around to ensure that the arrangement is built up evenly. This informal display is ideal for use with garden flowers as you can use any variety or color of blooms to create a charming arrangement.

We have used:
Aconitum
Peach Asiatic lilies
Peach carnations
Salal
Viburnum
Eucalyptus
Trachelium
Clear-glass vase with a waisted neck

1 Hold one tall stem of aconitum in your hand and surround it with several stems of salal foliage. This forms the center of the display – the aconitum should be slightly higher than the foliage.

2 Now add the peach lilies. Keep turning the arrangement in your hand to ensure that the lilies are positioned equidistantly.

Florist tip:
This arrangement would work equally well using only blue flowers, such as iris, statice or veronica, to complement the blue-gray eucalyptus foliage.

3 Continue to build up the arrangement in this way. Add more stems of aconitum, plus the viburnum, eucalyptus, and trachelium. Keep turning the arrangement in your hand to make sure it looks even on all sides. Finally, add the peach carnations. Hold the stems together firmly and slide into a tall, narrow-necked vase half-filled with water. If necessary, adjust the flowers and foliage to make an even display.

spring cascade

This stunning, asymmetric display reflects the colors of spring with elegant yellow calla lilies, pale orange gerbera, creamy–white lisianthus, and pure white antirrhinums against a background of fresh green leaves. The trailing pink amaranthus adds an accent of warm color. The arrangement is hand–tied, then placed in a tall glass vase. Plain containers work best as they do not draw the eye away from the flowers and foliage.

We have used:
Antirrhinum
Calla lilies
Gerbera
Lisianthus
Amaranthus
Ruscus
Ting ting
Raffia
Tall clear-glass vase with a wide neck

1 Hold several tall stems of white antirrhinums in one hand and surround with shorter-stemmed foliage. All the flowers should turn toward you as this is a forward-facing arrangement. Do not turn your hand as you build up the display.

Florist tip:
As a general rule, the height of the flowers should be 1¹/₂ times the height of the vase.

2 Add the yellow calla lilies at different heights, as shown in the picture. Place the gerbera in the center of the grouping. Add each stem at the same angle to ensure a spiral effect.

3 Add the cream lisianthus, then add the pink amaranthus and ruscus leaves to the front of the arrangement, allowing them to flow down. Finally, place a few ting ting stems at the back of the bunch to add height and interest. Tie the stems together with a length of raffia and place the arrangement in a tall vase half-filled with water. The amaranthus will drape gently over the edge of the vase and spill onto the surface below.

morning glow

*F**ull of bright summery sunshine yellows, this cheerful arrangement instantly lifts the soul. Greenery from the garden is mixed with buttery yellow roses and yellow pinhead proteas. These flowers are native to South Africa but are now widely available in flower shops and markets. However, if you can't track them down, spiky chrysanthemums would look equally good. Lotus seed heads also add a touch of the exotic.*

We have used:
Euonymus
Rosemary
Lotus seed heads
Yellow pinhead proteas
Yellow roses
Green ceramic vase

1 Fill the vase three-quarters full with water. Add the euonymus and rosemary foliage, creating a tall triangular shape. Keep the vase facing toward you as you add more foliage and flowers.

2 Continue to add more foliage to fill out the basic triangular form. Remember to strip away the lower leaves from the stems.

3 Add the tall stems of yellow proteas, evenly spacing them throughout the arrangement to add drama. Place the lotus seed heads at different heights to complement the bold shapes of the proteas. Finally, add the yellow roses in a group to the front of the vase, keeping the stems short.

springtime

*B*ring a touch of springtime color into your home with this fresh arrangement combining seasonal bulbs and garden greenery. Here we have included two types of narcissus – Paper Whites and Soleil d'Or – but you could use other varieties, such as the sweet-smelling Cheerfulness that are readily available at this time of year. Choose irises with small, neat flower heads to complement the delicacy of the narcissi.

We have used:
Eucalyptus
Asparagus fern
Soleil d'Or narcissi
Paper White narcissi
Blue iris
Heavy-based round clear-glass vase
with tapered neck

2 Add the tall stems of yellow Soleil d'Or narcissi. Their stems should be cut to different lengths to allow them to be dotted throughout the greenery, adding vibrant spots of color. Turn the vase as you do this to ensure that the arrangement looks good from all angles.

1 Half fill the vase with water. Arrange a generous quantity of asparagus fern and eucalyptus foliage in a fairly random manner, allowing some to splay out and gently droop over the edge of the vase for an informal look.

3 Fill in any gaps with the Paper White narcissi, also at various heights and positioned evenly throughout the arrangement. Finally, add the tall stems of blue iris to appear toward the top of the display.

citrus sensation

Contemporary arrangements don't simply rely on flowers to create an impact. Take inspiration from around the home – here we have plundered the kitchen and have used citrus fruits and sliced zucchini to add interest to the vase, but you could choose any fruits or vegetables to match your color scheme. This is a good trick to use at times of the year when flowers are less available or your favorite blooms are more expensive.

We have used:
Three stems of yellow Asiatic lilies
Two large fatsia japonica leaves
Lemons, limes and zucchini
Raffia
Tall cylindrical clear-glass vase

1 Strip all the lower leaves from the lily stems. Hold the three lily stems in one hand, twist the stems until the blooms are evenly spaced, then tie with a length of raffia a third of the way up the stems.

2 Place the lilies in the vase (do not fill it with water yet). Slice the lemons and limes into quarters (reserving one whole lemon for the final decoration). Cut the zucchini into thick slices, discarding the end pieces. Gently drop the zucchini slices and citrus quarters into the vase to anchor the stems in position. Fill the vase up to its brim, then use a jug to gently add water to the vase, taking care not to disturb the arrangement.

3 Add the two large fatsia leaves to the base of the arrangement to give balance to the tall lilies, taking care not to dislodge the flowers and fruits. Slice the reserved lemon in half and balance the halves on the fatsia leaves. If you wish, these can be wired into place. If your vase is displayed in a place where people may brush past it, it's a good idea to snip off the pollen-laden stamens as lily pollen is extremely prone to staining.

tulip elegance

*T*his sophisticated centerpiece is an ideal choice for dinner parties. The low-level design is stunning but allows guests to make easy conversation across the table. Anything too tall makes it awkward to serve food and can be distracting. Select blooms in shades to match or complement your chosen china and table linen. Pure white feathers introduce an additional decorative touch, their delicacy complementing the fine crystal glasses.

> **We have used:**
> *Several bunches of purple tulips*
> *Colored glass stones*
> *White feathers*
> *Decorative gold wire*
> *Wide-rimmed shallow glass bowl*

1 Fill the base of the bowl with a single layer of glass stones and add water to cover them. Cut the tulip stems to approximately half the width of the bowl, retaining as many leaves on the stems as possible. Lay the tulips loosely in an overlapping circle around the rim.

> **Florist tip:**
> *If you make the arrangement earlier in the day and place it somewhere warm, the tulips will have a chance to open before dinner is served.*

2 Add another layer of glass stones over the tulip stems to anchor them in place. Add the remaining tulips to fill any gaps, pushing the stems in between the stones. Add more water if necessary.

3 Cut off lengths of the decorative gold wire and twist them into loose spirals. Position on top of the tulips and stones. Add the feathers, radiating from the center to echo the curve of the tulips. Top with a few more wire spirals to finish.

eastern temple

*T*his striking vertical arrangement is created in horizontal layers, mixing exotic flowers and foliage with everyday blooms such as spray carnations. Floral foam allows you to construct this formal display with ease as it anchors the stems in place and keeps them moist. When selecting your flowers, choose a maximum of three colors and consider their position within the arrangement so the shades have equal impact.

We have used:
Two stems of straight bamboo
Tall orange celosia
Yellow spray carnations
Orange carthamus
Cream roses
Koala grass
Mini yellow-orange gerberas
Floral foam
Shallow ceramic dish

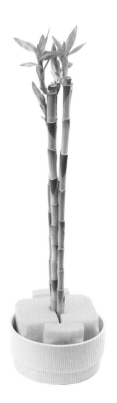

1 Cut the floral foam into blocks to fit the container and soak thoroughly in water. The foam needs to stand 1in above the top edge of the dish. Push the bamboo stems firmly into the center of the foam.

2 Cut the celosia stems so they are slightly shorter than the bamboo. Group them closely around the central bamboo to form the next layer of the arrangement, again pushing them firmly into the floral foam so they stay upright.

3 Continue to build up the separate layers, making sure that each layer is shorter than the one before. Make sure the final layer of gerberas covers the foam. Remember to top up the water in the bowl from time to time to ensure the foam doesn't dry out.

climbing lilies

Although this room is decorated in a classic style with traditional furnishings, this modern and sparse arrangement succeeds in creating a dramatic contrast. Oversized displays such as this work well when positioned in uncluttered settings where they can draw the eye. Here tall lengths of twisted willow are adorned with glass test tubes, which act as miniature vases for the elegant calla lilies.

We have used:
Twisted willow
Calla lilies
Leucadendron heads
Raffia
Glass test tubes
Copper wire
Short cylindrical glass vase

1 Half fill the vase with water and add the leucadendron heads. Make two 'H'-shaped frames out of the willow. Tie them together using short lengths horizontally between the verticals, near to their base. Bind tightly with raffia to secure. Place these around the vase (you may need someone to hold them) and bind additional horizontal lengths of willow to strengthen the framework.

2 Attach the glass test tubes to the willow framework by tying them securely in place with lengths of wire. Arrange the test tubes at various heights.

3 Using a jug, fill the test tubes with a little water. Gently thread the lilies through the willow framework and guide the base of their stems into the test tubes. Tie the lilies to the framework with raffia, just below the flower heads.

woodland wonder

Make the most of wintry woodland walks by collecting berries and foliage for use in indoor arrangements. Here stems of bright red holly berries introduce a welcome touch of vibrant color amongst silvery grey foliage. Fireplaces provide ideal settings for large-scale displays such as this. For the best effect, use a tall vase or a zinc container for this festive display.

We have used:
Silver eucalyptus
Santolina
Stems of red ilex (holly) berries
Cream Tokyo chrysanthemums
Silver ting ting
Tall ceramic vase

1 Three-quarters fill the vase with water. Prepare all the foliage by trimming the ends and stripping away any leaves from the lower part of the stems to prevent them rotting underwater. Arrange the eucalyptus foliage loosely in the vase.

2 Add the santolina foliage in amongst the eucalyptus to bulk up the display and fill any gaps. As this is a front-facing arrangement, there is no need to turn the vase and view the display from all sides.

Florist tip:
When using candles near flower displays, make sure there is no danger of any part of the arrangement catching alight and never leave lit candles unattended.

3 Place the ilex berries toward the center of the arrangement. Add the chrysanthemums and spirals of silver ting ting to complete.

Chapter 2
ice cool

forever blue

*F*lowers can provide an instant welcoming touch in any room of the house. Here a simple arrangement of freesias decorates a guest bathroom. In such a setting, keep the flowers uncomplicated so they don't take up more space than necessary. A final decorative touch is provided by the colored gravel, chosen to match the flowers. This gravel or sand can be bought from craft shops and floral suppliers.

We have used:
Lilac freesias
Colored gravel
Shallow oval glass vase

Florist tip:
If you cannot find colored gravel, colored glass nuggets or marbles make a good alternative.

1 Half fill the glass vase with the colored gravel, then three-quarters fill it with water. Trim any woody bits from the ends of the freesia stems, cutting all the stems to the same length. Push the first few stems into the gravel to create the outline of the arrangement.

2 Fill in the outline with the remaining freesias, creating a gentle arc shape across the top of the display. Remove any dead flower heads each day to encourage the remainder to open.

urban jungle

*T*hink beyond the obvious when arranging flowers. Almost any watertight container can be used – all you need is a little imagination. In this arrangement we have used a silver cake tin to great effect. Fluted brioche tins or rectangular loaf tins would work equally well. This display is built up in quarters to ensure it looks good from all sides. Keep turning the container as you add more flowers and foliage – to check the effect.

We have used:
Three stems of cyperus papyrus
Two stems of curly bamboo
Two fatsia japonica leaves
Two lime-green chrysanthemums
Six hosta leaves
Four lotus seed heads
Santini (miniature chrysanthemums)
Carpet moss
Floral foam
Raffia
Wire pins
Round silver cake tin with a solid base

1 Cut the floral foam into blocks to fill the cake tin, then soak them well in water. Cut the stems of cyperus papyrus to three different heights, then place them in the center of the foam blocks. Gather up the fronds and tie them halfway along their length with raffia.

2 Trim the straight ends from the bamboo and reserve them for later. Add the curly bamboo stems to the foam. Add fatsia leaves to opposite sides of the cake tin, securing them in the foam with a wire pin, and place a chrysanthemum head just above them, pushing the stem into the foam. Cover the remaining foam with carpet moss and secure it with a wire pin.

3 Add the reserved lengths of bamboo to the arrangement as shown, then arrange the lotus seed heads at varying heights. Add the hosta leaves and the santini to cover any remaining foam.

sheer elegance

For restrained elegance, the gracious lily simply cannot be surpassed. Just a few tall stems in a stylish vase can create the most sophisticated of arrangements. In fact, these long-lasting flowers are best left to shine on their own rather than being hidden amongst other blooms. Available all year round, the glorious longiflorum lilies used here have a beautiful fragrance which will scent an entire room.

We have used:
*Curly silver ting ting
Longiflorum lilies
Waisted clear-glass vase with
a wide neck*

Florist tip:
Do not cut out the stamens of lilies, but gently pull the pollen sacks off the stamens with your fingertips. If cut, the stamens will turn brown.

1 Half fill the vase with water. Carefully place the curly ends of the ting ting in the water (ie use it upside-down). Splay out the straight ends evenly around the vase and trim to different heights.

2 Trim the ends of the lily stems and remove any lower leaves. Carefully remove the stamens from any open buds (this is because the pollen stains easily). Add lilies to the vase one by one, positioning the stems evenly between the ting ting.

3 Add the remaining lilies and top up the water level to reach the neck of the vase. Carefully rotate the vase to ensure that the arrangement looks good from all angles. Trim the ting ting if necessary. As the buds open over the next few days, continue to remove the stamens.

rock pool

This striking, contemporary arrangement is unusual because it features water plants positioned above the water line and mini gerbera happily submerged within the glass tank. This method of display proves that floral arrangements don't always have to look natural – here the brightly colored bands of sand and silver-coated shells add an exotic, almost surreal, quality to the watery still life.

We have used:
Water plants
Two mini gerbera
Gravel or sand in several different colors
Large shells
Gold wire
Tall clear-glass tank

1 Tilt the tank to one side and spoon in a layer of sand. Holding the tank steady, carefully spoon in another layer. Take care not to shake the vase to avoid mixing the layers. Continue building up different colored layers. The final layer should have a level surface. Pour the water in from a jug, letting it trickle over your hand to prevent a forceful jet disturbing the sand.

2 Carefully lower the shells into the tank, resting one on top of the other. Carefully add more water if necessary.

3 Lower the water plant into the tank, ensuring all its roots are submerged. Tie the two gerberas together, facing in opposite directions, by wrapping a short length of wire around the stems, trimming the stems if necessary. Carefully lower them into the water so they float beneath the water plant. Add more water so the plant is level with the rim of the tank.

country classic

The perfect arrangement for a mixed bunch of blooms gathered from a summer garden. This classic creation makes an imposing display, ideal for an entrance hall. You could recreate this look using whatever is available in your border, just make sure you include some tall varieties – here delphiniums have been used to great effect but larkspur, lupins, iris, or gladioli would work just as well.

We have used:
Salal
Ruscus
Delphiniums in shades of blue
White lisianthus
Purple-pink celosia
Pale pink roses
Conical clear-glass vase with
a flared neck

1 Half fill the vase with water. Add a generous amount of salal and ruscus foliage, rotating the vase as each stem is added to ensure that it looks good from all angles.

Florist tip:
Try to be adventurous in your choice of container. For a different look, arrange the same selection of flowers and foliage in a solid white ceramic tank. This instantly gives the display a more modern and graphic appearance suited to a contemporary interior.

2 Now add all the long-stemmed flowers, placing them evenly throughout the foliage to ensure a good shape and blend of colors. Add the stems of celosia. Trim some of the rose stems to shorter lengths and place them around the lower edges of the vase. The taller stemmed roses can be placed in the center of the arrangement.

steps to heaven

This fun and quirky approach to flower arranging shows how to make just a few blooms go a long way. Inexpensive colored foam is cut to fit within a family of glass tanks, creating a stripey effect. The bubblegum-bright colors bring a youthful touch to classic roses. This quick-to-create arrangement would be perfect for a guest bedroom. Single heads of gerberas or ranunculi would also look terrific.

We have used:
*Three or four rosebuds per tank, in a mixture of colors and with leaves attached to the stems
Multi-pack of different colored foam
Curling ribbon
Wire pins
Family of three glass tanks*

2 Add leaves around the rose. Larger tanks can accommodate several rosebuds, but these should be grouped within one corner for the best visual effect.

1 Cut the foam to fit within the three tanks. Each foam layer needs to be approximately ³/₄in thick. Vary the order of the colors within each tank. Pour sufficient water into each tank to ensure that all layers are saturated. Shorten the rose stems and insert a rose into the smallest tank – you may need to use a skewer to create a channel for the stem.

3 Cut short lengths of curling ribbon and pin in place close to the rosebuds, allowing the ribbon to drape over the edges of the tanks.

sunflower bouquet

The cheerful, almost childlike simplicity of summer sunflowers is guaranteed to bring an instant smile to anyone's face. Most children have tried growing these glorious flowers at some time, measuring the rapidly growing stems against their own height. In this project sunflowers are given a touch of sophistication by grouping four flower heads into a bouquet surrounded by the glossiest of aspidistra leaves.

We have used:
Four sunflowers
Aspidistra leaves
Curling ribbon
Shears
Shallow glass bowl with a wide neck

1 Hold one sunflower in your hand about 4in down from the flower head. Place the first aspidistra leaf at the back of the sunflower and gently fold the leaf tip down into your hand. Hold this firmly. Add another three leaves evenly around the sunflower and repeat the folding process.

2 Add the remaining three sunflowers to the bunch. Surround these with more leaves, folding them down as before. The leaves form the outer edge of the bunch and separate the sunflowers from one another.

3 Holding the bunch firmly, cut all the stems to the depth of the vase, using sharp shears. Tie firmly with a length of curling ribbon. Place in the water-filled vase. If you wish, the vase can also be filled with exotic fruits, such as lychees or ornamental seed pods.

Florist tip:
Before starting this arrangement, wipe the aspidistra leaves with a soft damp cloth to remove any dust.

tall tower

his is a truly modern arrangement without a flower in sight. The tall, clean lines of the snake grass are almost sculptural in appearance, while the warm red rosehips create a neat collar around the top of the vase. This display demands to take center stage and would look perfect in an entrance hall. For a softer, more feminine look, simply replace the rosehips with a circlet of scented flowers.

We have used:
Snake grass
Rosehips
Shears
Raffia
Hessian ribbon
Wire pins
Clear-glass vase with a flared neck

1 Make a large bundle of snake grass by grouping stems together in one hand. All the grasses should be the same length, so trim them with shears as necessary.

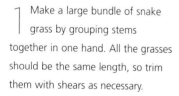

Florist tip:
If snake grass is unavailable, try using straight bamboo canes instead.

2 Tie the bundle together about 3in from the base with a length of raffia. Cover the raffia with a neat band of hessian ribbon, securing it in place with wire pins. Stand the snake grass in the vase and fill with water to just below the level of the band of hessian.

3 Trim the rosehip stems and place them around the snake grass. Bind the top of the snake grass bundle with raffia 4in from the top.

Chapter 3
hot favorites

wildly exotic

*T*he dramatic contortions of twisted willow contrast magnificently with the vivid colors of the daisy-like gerberas. These flowers are now widely available all year round in a fantastic array of colors. Here we have used a mixture of paintbox-bright shades to create a cheerful and eye-catching display. This arrangement perfectly demonstrates how two completely different ingredients can work well in harmony.

We have used:
Twisted willow
Large gerberas in assorted colors
Raffia
Gourds
Clear-glass vase with flared neck

Florist tip:
Gerbera stems can sometimes be a little limp, so it may be necessary to strengthen them by carefully coiling a length of florist's wire around the stem, right up to the flower head.

1 Three-quarters fill the vase with water. Tie the stems of willow together with raffia to make an effective shape, then place them in the vase. The raffia should be just above the waterline.

2 Add the red gerberas, trimming the stems to various heights and turning the vase to check the profile from all angles. Add the other gerberas, leaving enough space between them to be able to see each individual flower head. Add a couple of decorative gourds around the neck of the vase for extra interest.

valentine roses

Who can deny the romance of receiving a dozen red roses on Valentine's Day? These classic flowers demand to be displayed center stage. Pack a vase with assorted green foliage to emphasize their color and beauty. The deep wine-red roses used here are a touch more sophisticated than their scarlet sisters. Place them where they can be admired by all.

We have used:
Three aspidistra leaves
Bupleurum foliage
Umbrella fern
Twelve long-stemmed deep red roses
Clear-glass vase with a slightly flared neck

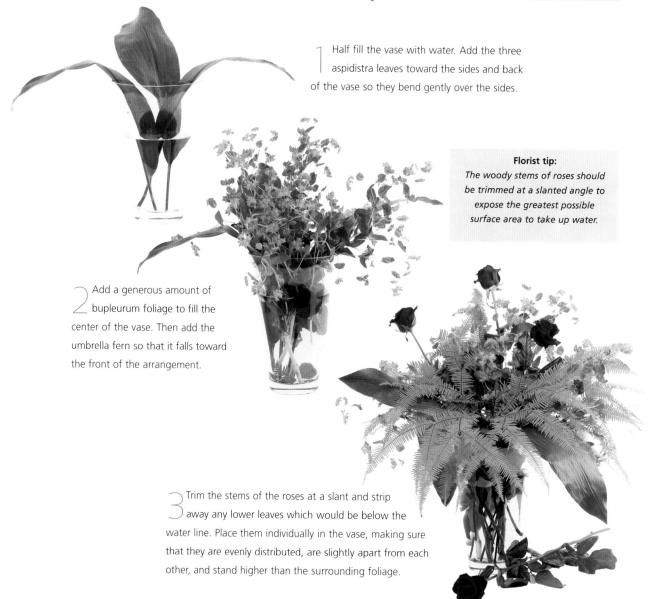

1 Half fill the vase with water. Add the three aspidistra leaves toward the sides and back of the vase so they bend gently over the sides.

Florist tip:
The woody stems of roses should be trimmed at a slanted angle to expose the greatest possible surface area to take up water.

2 Add a generous amount of bupleurum foliage to fill the center of the vase. Then add the umbrella fern so that it falls toward the front of the arrangement.

3 Trim the stems of the roses at a slant and strip away any lower leaves which would be below the water line. Place them individually in the vase, making sure that they are evenly distributed, are slightly apart from each other, and stand higher than the surrounding foliage.

oriental simplicity

*T*his cleanly modern and geometric arrangement of snake grass and gerbera is reminiscent of the ancient Japanese art of flower display known as ikebana. This composition needs a degree of forward planning as all the elements have to work in perfect harmony. A simple container with clean lines and a minimalist, uncluttered setting are also required to show this creation off to full advantage.

We have used:
Snake grass
Red mini gerberas
Carpet moss
Floral foam
Wire pins
Black polished pebbles
Shallow container

1 Fill the container with soaked floral foam. Build up the snake grass framework. Position several tall lengths of snake grass on the left side, pushing them securely into the foam. Add two short lengths either side and two medium lengths to the right of the container.

Florist tip:
The floral foam needs to stand about 2in proud of the container's edge to allow enough room to accommodate the horizontal stems.

2 Create the horizontal lines. Add several medium lengths of snake grass to the front, back, and left sides of the foam, and several longer pieces to the right side of the container. When viewed from above, the horizontal stems of snake grass should resemble a cross.

3 Cover the foam with a blanket of carpet moss, pinned into position. Take the tallest gerbera, push it into the foam alongside the tallest grouping of snake grass. Add the other vertical gerberas in the same way. Then add the horizontal gerberas. Place a few polished pebbles on the carpet moss.

evening glow

*E*legant candles surrounded by an abundant collar of foliage create a festive welcome for winter guests. Here we have used an attractive combination of mixed garden foliage in varying shades of green with interesting leaf bracts and colorful berries. Also keep an eye out in florists for more unusual foliage imported from warmer climates. This low-level arrangement would work very well as a table center.

We have used:
Mixed foliage, such as hypericum, snowberries, bupleurum and eucalyptus
Two tall candles (choose a color to match the berries)
Two candle holders
Floral foam
Shallow circular container

1 Cut the floral foam to fit snugly within the container. It should be approximately twice the height of the container. Soak the foam well and place it in the dish. Insert the candles into the holders and push them into the center of the foam.

2 Cut the foliage into short sprays and build up the display around the sides and over the top in small groups, ensuring a good mix of colors, berries, and leaf shapes.

3 Continue in this way, making sure the foam is fully covered. Also ensure that the sides of the container are hidden. To encourage the arrangement to last, top up the container with a little water from time to time and mist the foliage regularly with a fine spray of water. Do make sure, however, that the spray does not damage any wooden surfaces below the container.

For your safety
• *Although candles and flowers are perfect partners, remember to make sure there is no danger of any part of the arrangement catching alight.*
• *Never leave candles unattended and always ensure that they are fully extinguished before you leave the room.*
• *See page 4 for full safety instructions before using candle arrangements.*

tropical delight

This lush arrangement of vibrant pink proteas will bring back memories of vacations in exotic places where exuberant flowers and foliage like this grow in the wild. This method of assembling the flowers in the hand and then tying them as a bouquet is a very easy and popular technique. The resulting arrangement can either be placed in a vase or wrapped in bright tissue paper and cellophane and given as a gift.

We have used:
Four pink proteas
Assorted tropical foliage,
including ferns, leucadendron,
and monstera leaves
Eucalyptus
String
Clear-glass vase with a
waisted neck

1 Begin grouping the flowers in your hand. Start with one protea placed centrally and surround it with other large foliage and flowers. Keep turning the bouquet in your hand as you add more, to ensure that it looks good from all sides.

2 Add the remaining three proteas equidistantly around the bouquet and surround them with smaller-leaved foliage, such as stems of eucalyptus. Remember to rotate the bouquet to ensure an even arrangement.

3 Finally, add a couple of spiky palm leaves around the outer edges of the bouquet. Tie the bouquet firmly with a length of string. Trim the stems to similar lengths. Half fill the vase with water and place the bouquet in it.

Florist tip:
If some of your chosen foliage has extremely thick stems, to make it easier to hold the bouquet during assembly, simply add these stems directly to the vase once the bouquet is in place.

wreathed bouquet

This unusual arrangement comprises two separate elements: a delicate wreath made from trailing ivy and viburnum berries, plus a hand-tied bouquet of red lilies and salal leaves. The wreath sits on the neck of the vase, providing a neat collar for the bouquet. Arrange the lily bouquet so that the open flowers rest on the ivy circle, while the unopened buds stand proud. The wreath can be made to fit any size of vase or container.

We have used:
Long lengths of trailing ivy
Sprigs of viburnum with berries
Red Asiatic lilies
Salal leaves
Silver reel wire
Parafilm
Curling ribbon
Clear-glass vase with a waisted neck

1 Cut a length of wire to form a circle slightly larger than the neck of the vase. Twist the ends together and cover the join of the wire with parafilm.

2 Wrap long lengths of ivy around the wire circle to form a delicate wreath, weaving them up and over the wire to secure them in place.

3 Cut the viburnum into small sprays and wire it into place equidistantly around the ivy circlet. Make sure that all the leaves lie in one direction and cover the bare stems, and that the berries fall to the outer edge of the circle.

4 Gather the lilies in one hand to make a neat bouquet and surround with salal. Tie with ribbon and trim the stems. Half fill the vase with water and place the wreath around the neck. Add a few long stems of ivy to trail down. Carefully insert the lily bouquet into the vase.

touch of romance

A simple arrangement of flowers in shades of just one color can create great impact. Here the tones of pink range from baby pink tulips through to deep cerise gerberas, with roses and lilies providing other touches of pink along the way. Placed in front of a dressing table mirror, all sides of this hand-tied bouquet are visible, and the scent of the roses and lilies will drift across the room. Cut the stems so that the flower heads rest just above the rim of the vase for an ideal effect.

We have used:
Three pink lilies
Six pink roses
Five large cerise pink gerberas
Six pale pink tulips
Umbrella fern
Eucalyptus
Salal leaves
Raffia
Flared clear glass vase

1 Strip the lower leaves from the lily and rose stems. Gather the lily stems together in one hand, rotating the stems until you achieve an even spread of flowers.

2 Add the umbrella fern around the lilies, then place the roses in the bouquet. Keep turning the arrangement in your hand to ensure that it looks symmetrical.

3 Add the eucalyptus foliage, then the gerberas, and finally the tulips. Tie with a length of raffia, just below the flower heads. Trim the stems so they are the same length. Half fill the vase with water and carefully position the bouquet.

Florist tip:
Remember that lily pollen can stain. If you wish, carefully pull the pollen sacks off the stamens of any open blooms to stop pollen falling on the table or carpet.

rainforest find

Coloring the water within a clear-glass vase adds an unexpected twist to this exotic arrangement. Simply add a few drops of food coloring to the vase and see how it changes the overall look of the display. Snake grass is very useful in flower arranging as it can be bent into various shapes to add a geometric look. If anthuriums are not available, arum lilies or amaryllis would look just as magnificent.

We have used:
Snake grass
Umbrella fern
Five pink anthuriums
Pink food coloring
Raffia
Tall clear-glass vase

1 Take three long stems of snake grass and bend the top halves into triangular shapes. Secure these with raffia and set to one side. Hold the remaining snake grass in one hand, with the tips at varying heights. Surround with the umbrella fern.

2 Add the triangular snake grass stems to the front of the hand-held bunch. This is a front-facing arrangement so you do not need to rotate it in your hand to check the visual effect.

Florist tip:
Choose a shade of food coloring to match the flowers or the room decor.

3 Add the pink anthuriums in a staggered line, all facing toward the front. Add more umbrella ferns toward the back of the bouquet. Tie the bouquet with raffia. Three-quarters fill the vase with water and add a few drops of pink food coloring. Stir the water to mix the color evenly, then add the bouquet.

kitchen garden

*P*erfect for a kitchen worktop, this terracotta pot holds a bounty of aromatic herbs, pungent chilies and garlic cloves. All the ingredients used here can be found in the kitchen garden or the larder, apart from the deep blue anemones which add a vibrant touch of color. In the summer months, you could reinforce the herb theme by replacing the anemones with purple borage flowers, pink chives, or orange nasturtiums.

We have used:
Sprays of mixed herbs, such as rosemary, bay, and dill flower heads
Euonymus foliage
Blue anemones
One clementine
Two garlic bulbs
Two large red chilies
Short twigs
Reel wire
Terracotta pot

1 Half fill the terracotta pot with water and pack it full of herbs and euonymus foliage. Turn the pot as you do this to ensure that it looks good from all sides. Include a few taller spikes of rosemary to add height.

2 Add the blue anemones throughout the foliage. Push one twig firmly into the clementine. Attach twigs to the garlic bulbs with lengths of wire. Add these to the center of the arrangement.

3 Wire the chili stems together and attach to a twig. Push them into the terracotta bowl so they hang down over the lip of the bowl. Add some sprays of dill flowers to complete.

Florist tip:
Chilies can cause skin irritation, so take care when handling them. Make sure that you wash your hands afterwards and do not rub your eyes.

Chapter 4

pastel palette

green goddess

*T*he arum lilies used in this arrangement are a variety known as 'Green Goddess.' Their tall, sculptural shape provides the perfect foil for the wispy bear grass and the soft, trailing amaranthus. The large monstera leaf adds body to the back of the display. Arum lily stems tend to split and curl at the ends after a few days so do trim them regularly to make the most of these long-lasting flowers.

We have used:
Five arum lilies
Bear grass
One large monstera leaf
Green amaranthus
Colored sand or gravel
Clear-glass vase with a narrow neck

1 Fill the vase with a layer of colored sand or gravel. Add water to a level three-quarters of the way up the vase. Pour the water in carefully to avoid disturbing the sand or gravel layer. Add the bear grass, allowing it to cascade down over the edges of the vase.

2 Add the first arum lily, pushing the stem down to rest on the sand or gravel layer.

3 Add the remaining lilies, making sure that they are evenly spaced and face in different directions. Add the monstera leaf at the back of the vase and position the green amaranthus to trail down over the front.

whispering tulips

*S*implicity is the key to this modern arrangement of spring bulbs. Oversized vases can be used to great effect with small-scale flowers, as demonstrated by the tulips enclosed within this curvaceous vase. For the best results, choose tulips with a subtle streaked pattern – this prevents the flowers merging into one mass of color. This technique could also be used with flowers such as narcissi, iris, freesias, or forsythia.

We have used:
*Pale pink tulips
Tall clear-glass vase with a wide neck, preferably with an interestingly shaped lip*

1 Fill the vase with water to a depth of about 2in. Remove the leaves from all the tulips. Cut the stems of a third of the tulips to about 2in in length. Cut the stems of another third to about 5in and the remaining third to about 8in so that they fit just below the rim of the vase.

Florist tip:
Because of the style of this arrangement, the vase holds very little water. Check the water level regularly and carefully top it up when necessary. It is best to pour additional water through a funnel to avoid soaking the flower heads.

2 Place the shortest tulips carefully at the bottom of the vase with the flower heads grouped toward the center of the vase.

3 Arrange the medium-length tulips in the vase with their stems outside the inner circle of short flowers. Finally, add the tallest tulips with their stems positioned in the center of the vase.

eastern promise

*O*rchid flowers are very long-lasting, so although they may seem like an indulgence to buy, they will provide weeks of pleasure. The delicacy of the blooms is accentuated by the robust fatsia leaves. Various garden shrubs, such as cornus, boast glorious red canes during the winter months and these can be used in indoor arrangements. When choosing which stems to cut, select young stems which are easier to bend.

We have used:
Long lengths of red twigs
Three stems of cymbidium orchids
Two fatsia japonica leaves
Curling ribbon
Straight-sided clear-glass vase with a wide neck

1 Three-quarters fill the vase with water. Cut some small pieces of red twig and place them in the vase below the water line.

2 Hold a tall stem of orchids in one hand and group several tall red twigs around the back and sides of the flowers. Add the second orchid stem at the front of the bouquet, slightly lower than the first, and add the third stem at right angles to the first one, so that it points out to the side.

3 Add the large fatsia leaves at the base of the orchids to give balance. Tie the bouquet securely with a length of curling ribbon just below the fatsia leaves, and place in the vase, with the bouquet stems sitting in amongst the submerged red twigs.

soft focus

Gypsophila, or baby's breath as it is commonly known, has a mass of frothy, delicate white flowers, perfect for covering a foam ring. When used horizontally as part of a table setting, floral wreaths make wonderful candle surrounds. Small glass storm lanterns are ideal when used in combination with wreaths as the candle flame is safely contained. This arrangement would be perfect for a christening lunch.

We have used:
Large quantity of gypsophila
Floral foam ring on a base
Sand
Glass storm lantern
Large cream pillar candle

1 Add a small amount of sand to the storm lantern. This will provide a heavy base in which the candle can safely rest. Add the candle – it should be slightly shorter than the height of the storm lantern.

2 Soak the foam ring thoroughly. The container below will provide a reservoir to catch any excess water. Cut the gypsophila into small sprays.

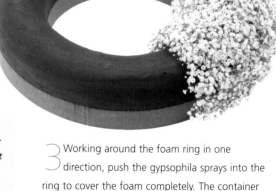

For your safety
• Although candles and flowers are perfect partners, remember to make sure there is no danger of any part of the arrangement catching alight.
• Never leave candles unattended and always ensure that they are fully extinguished before you leave the room.
• See page 4 for full safety instructions before using candle arrangements.

3 Working around the foam ring in one direction, push the gypsophila sprays into the ring to cover the foam completely. The container should also be hidden from view. Place the wreath in position and add the storm lantern to the center.

tall elegance

*B*ear grass creates a wonderful fountain-like effect *flowing from the top of this tall vase. The narrow neck of the vase holds the arrangement securely in place, making a neat posy of roses and foliage. If your garden is bereft of roses, try using ranunculi, anemones, or any other flowers with tight, rounded heads. Frosted glass has a cool, almost icy appearance well suited to this clean and contemporary interior.*

We have used:
*Long-stemmed roses in a variety
of pastel shades
Bear grass
Salal leaves
Curling ribbon
Tall, slim frosted-glass vase with
a narrow neck*

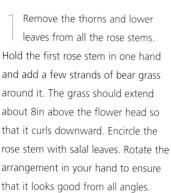

1 Remove the thorns and lower leaves from all the rose stems. Hold the first rose stem in one hand and add a few strands of bear grass around it. The grass should extend about 8in above the flower head so that it curls downward. Encircle the rose stem with salal leaves. Rotate the arrangement in your hand to ensure that it looks good from all angles.

2 Continue to build up the arrangement in this way, adding roses and bear grass. Add another layer of salal leaves interspersed with bear grass around the outer edges of the bouquet.

3 Tie the arrangement with a length of curling ribbon just below the outer leaves. Keep the stems long, but trim them so that they are all even. Half fill the vase with water and carefully insert the bouquet. You may need to hold the stems together tightly to feed them through the narrow neck of the vase.

rose garden

T *his neat white cube looks like a gift box just waiting to be opened. Once you have assembled all the elements, this arrangement is quick and easy to put together as it only features four roses, twisted willow, and some fresh green fern. A central core of floral foam is disguised under a blanket of pure white gravel. You could also pack moss around the foam for a more natural effect, or shells for a seaside look.*

We have used:
Pale pink roses
Umbrella fern
Twisted willow
Floral foam
White gravel
Square glass tank

1 Cut a small block of floral foam to fit within the tank. The top should be level with the upper edge of the glass. Soak the foam thoroughly. Put a layer of white gravel in the base of the vase and place the damp foam on top in the center. Carefully fill the gaps around all four sides with more gravel. Also cover the top of the foam with a thin layer of gravel.

2 Strip the leaves from the rose stems and trim to a length of about 3in. Push the stem of the first rose into the foam at a slight angle so that it faces forward and the petals rest on the gravel.

3 Add two more roses in the same way, also facing outward. Add another rose to the center of the arrangement with its head pointing vertically and positioned slightly higher than the others. Add sprigs of fern between the roses and a couple of tall twigs of twisted willow to the back of the display.

simply sophisticated

*P*ure green and white is a classic combination which can be enjoyed at any time of the year. The cool, calming hues are perfectly suited for a sophisticated supper table and echo the colors of the china and glassware. Resist the temptation to introduce any other colors as this would dilute the stylish effect. Choose lilies with a subtle scent so that they do not overwhelm the mouthwatering aromas of the food.

We have used:
White lilies
September flower
Euonymus
Bear grass
Fatsia japonica leaf
Aspidistra leaf
Raffia
Clear-glass vase with a wide neck

1 Strip the lower leaves from the lily stems. Take a stem of lily in one hand and place some sprigs of September flower behind. Turn the arrangement in your hand to ensure that it looks good from all sides, then continue to add more lilies and September flowers.

2 Surround the bouquet with a layer of euonymus foliage. Place the large fatsia leaf to one side of the bouquet. Add some strands of bear grass, bending the tips down and grasping them with the stems to create an arc.

3 Add more bear grass to the bouquet, bending some strands back as before and allowing some to trail down. Position the aspidistra leaf opposite the fatsia leaf. Tie the bouquet securely with a length of raffia just below the leaves. Half fill the vase with water and place the bouquet in it.

oriental beauty

*O*rchids always look best in simple designs where their delicate flowers and striking beauty can be fully appreciated. Here we have used pure white and striped purple and white varieties, but other colorways would look just as stunning. The simple mechanics of this arrangement are concealed by a covering of gray-green moss. Orchids do not require a large amount of water so the foam-filled cup and water phial suits them well.

We have used:
Phalaenopsis orchids in white and purple
Moss
Bear grass
Plastic cup
Water phial
Floral foam
Silver wire
Pale blue glass nuggets
Shallow glass bowl

1 Fill the plastic cup with floral foam and soak with water. Cover the outside of the plastic cup with moss, binding it in place with silver wire. Cut off one stem of the orchid flowers; place the stem in the damp floral foam and cover the foam with moss to conceal it, binding it in the same way. Place an orchid in the water phial and also disguise it with moss.

2 Place the moss-covered water phial containing the orchid in the bowl and add a few pale blue glass nuggets. Carefully position the moss-covered cup in the neck of the bowl.

3 Place the remaining orchid stems and bear grass in the foam, pushing the stems down well to anchor them securely in the cup. One of the orchid stems should be cut short and arranged to trail down over the edge of the bowl.

formal splendor

*T*his show-stopping arrangement demands space
and would look fantastic in an entrance hall to
greet guests at a party. The oversized glass flute is the
last word in elegance and deserves to be partnered with
classic white Casablanca lilies. Select lilies and foliage
with the longest stems possible to add balance to the
design. Make sure you keep the vase topped off with
water to allow the lily buds to open.

We have used:
Casablanca lilies
Bear grass
Monstera leaves
Twisted willow
Small decorative stones or
glass beads
Raffia
Extra tall clear-glass vase

1 Add a little water to the vase, then hold it at an angle and slide the stones or beads in. You must do this gently to avoid breaking the glass. The stones will add ballast to the vase and will provide stability. Using a jug, gently pour in more water to come two-thirds of the way up the vase. Strip the lower leaves from the lily stems. Hold one lily stem in your hand and surround it with strands of bear grass.

2 Add the remaining lily stems and bear grass to the bouquet, rotating it in your hand to make sure that it looks good from all sides. Position the twisted willow toward the back to add height and interest. Place the monstera leaves at the base of the bouquet and tie securely with a length of raffia. Trim the stems level and place carefully in the vase. Make sure the vase is level and is in no danger of being knocked over.